CARLOS CHAVEZ

Cuatro Estudios
Four Piano Etudes
(1919-21)

Edited by Max Lifchitz

Carlanita Music Company (ASCAP)
Sole Selling Agent: G. Schirmer, Inc,. New York

Carlos Chávez was born in México City on June 13, 1899. Active as composer, pianist, conductor, educator, writer and arts administrator, he was the indisputable leader of México's musical life for over 50 years. Chávez raised México's musical standards and exerted a tremendous influence on every facet of that country's artistic life. He died in 1978 at the age of 79.

Carlos Chávez learned the rudiments of music from his elder brother Manuel. He continued his studies under the supervision of the composer Manuel M. Ponce (1910-14) and the pianist Pedro Luis Ogazón (1915-20). Although his mentors introduced him to the classical and romantic repertoire, the young composer made every effort to keep up with the new music being written in the European capitals during the early years of the 20th century.

Prior to 1921, when the Mexican government commissioned him to write the ballet *El Fuego Nuevo* (The New Fire), Chávez had written a considerable amount of piano and chamber music. Overly demanding and self-critical, he classified these works as "juvenilia" and did not allow their publication. Fortunately, thanks to the efforts of Mrs. Ana Chávez, the composer's daughter, the early works of this important musical figure are reaching the public for the first time.

The *Cuatro Estudios* (Four Piano Etudes) were written when Chávez was experimenting with the pianistic style created by the romantic composers. While the music of the *Cuatro Estudios* lacks any overt nationalistic flavor, it already manifests stylistic signs often found in Chávez's mature works including a great sense of shape, boldness in its conception and endless vitality.

The *Cuatro Estudios* speak of a romanticism without voluptuousness. The music reveals a composer influenced by the romanticism of Robert Schumann and Frederic Chopin but also aware of the modernism of Claude Debussy. The harmonic language employs numerous unusual chord formations and surprising modulations throughout. The pianistic writing is at the same time complex and diverse, providing the performer with ample opportunity for display of technical virtuosity.

This edition was prepared following the composer's manuscripts carefully. While metronomic tempi were added by the editor, most other markings follow the original manuscript as closely as possible.

Pianists will enjoy the many technical challenges found in these intriguing compositions. Music lovers will find enormous pleasure discovering these imaginative works by one of the truly important figures of 20th century music.

Max Lifchitz
New York, 1992

Estudio I

Carlos Chávez [1919]

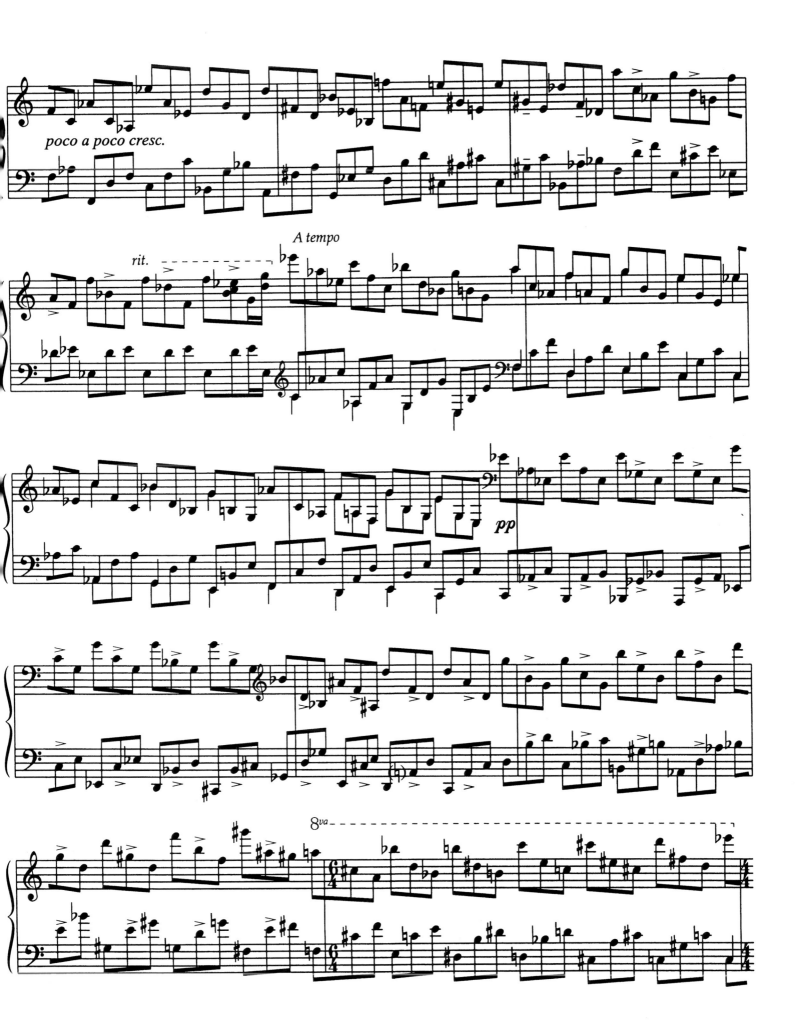

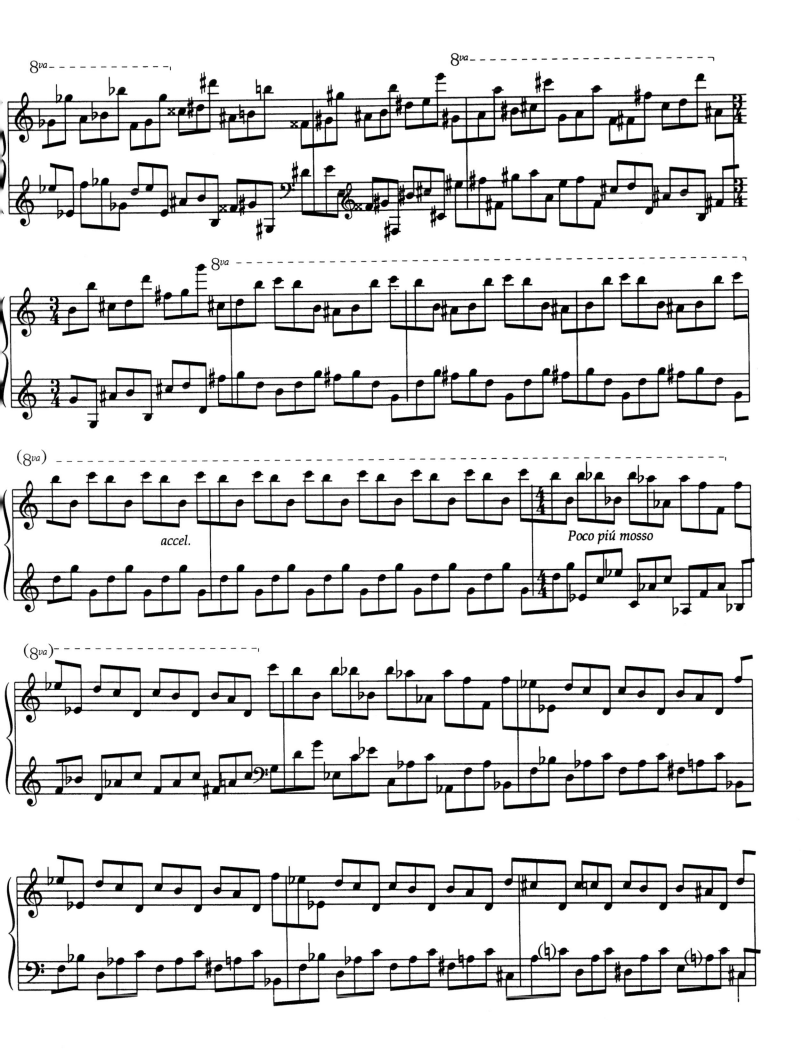

poco a poco rall.

Tempo I

poco a poco rit e dim

ppp

Estudio II

Carlos Chávez[1919]

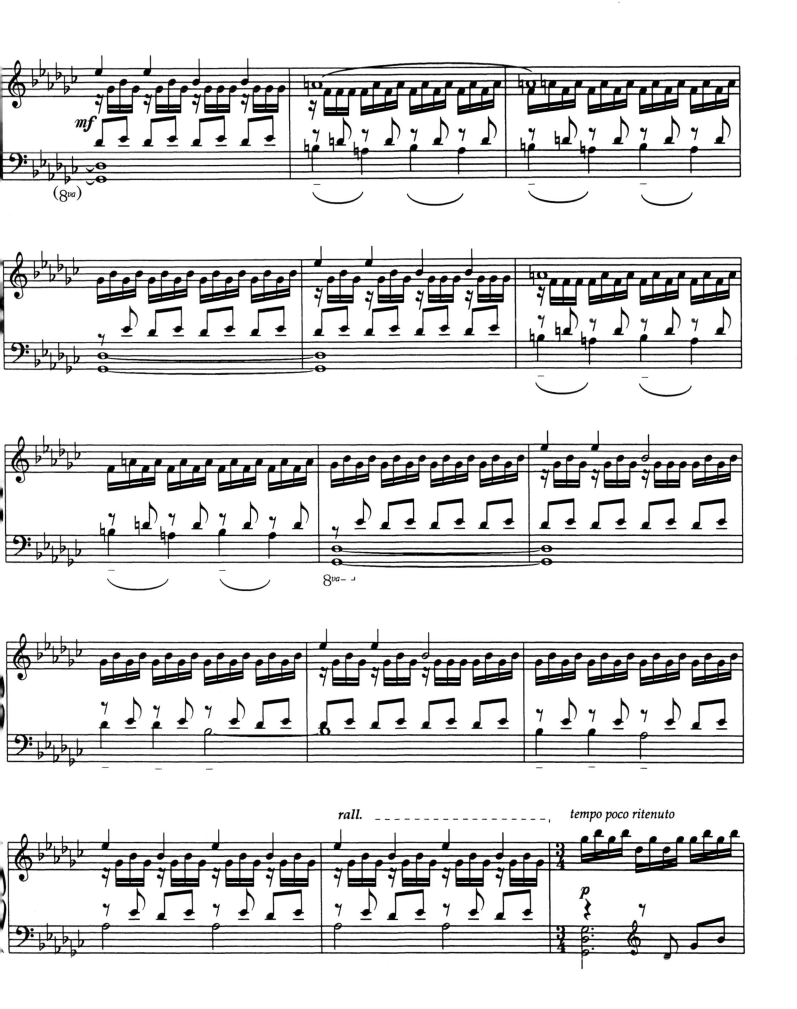

rall. _ *tempo poco ritenuto*

Estudio III

Carlos Chávez[1920]

Moderato Cantabile (♩ = ca.116)

poco a poco dim

Estudio IV

A Ignaz Friedman

Carlos Chávez [1921]

Allegro Fluido (♩ = ca. 132)

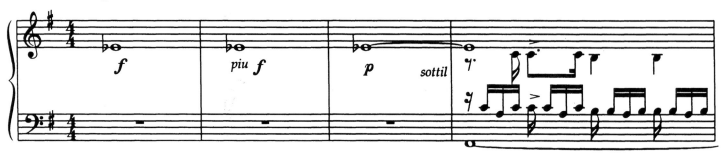

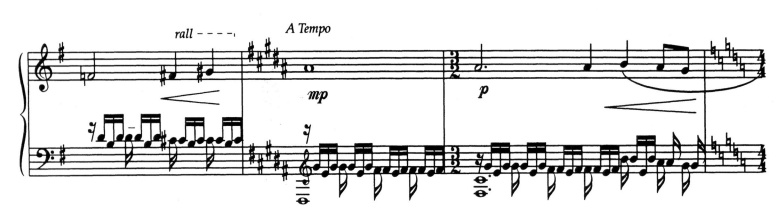

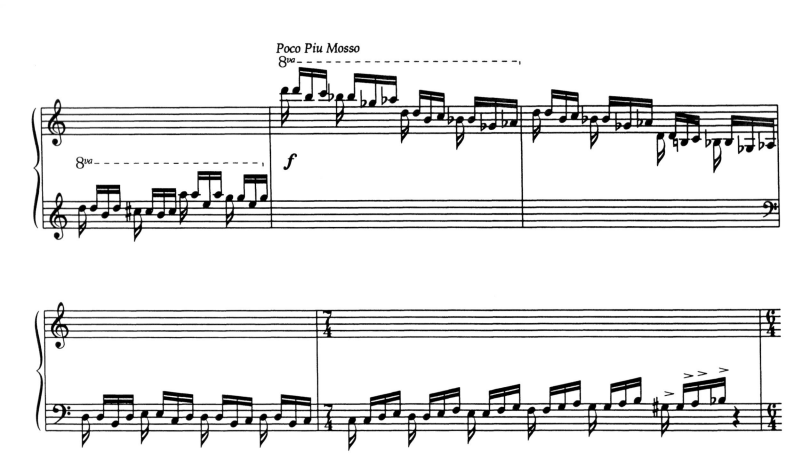

Poco Piu Mosso

f

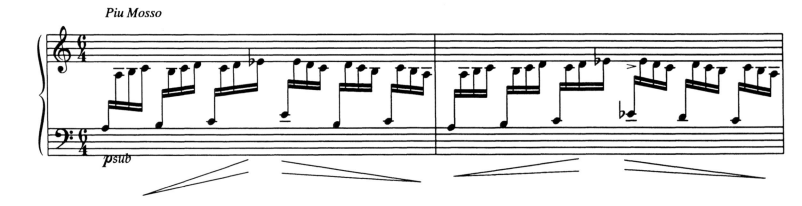

Piu Mosso

p sub

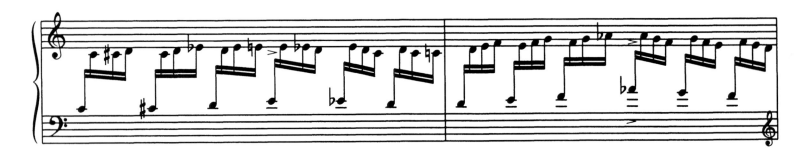

poco a poco cresc.

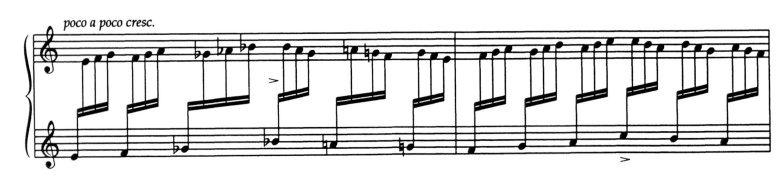

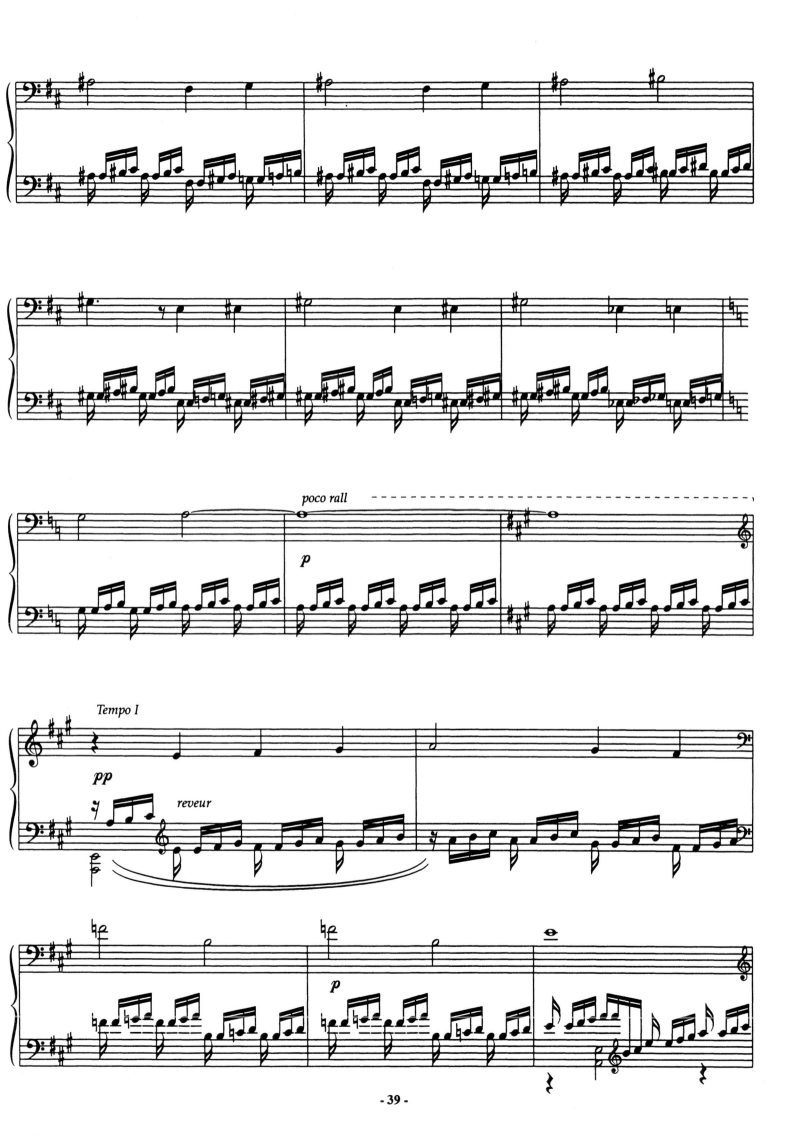

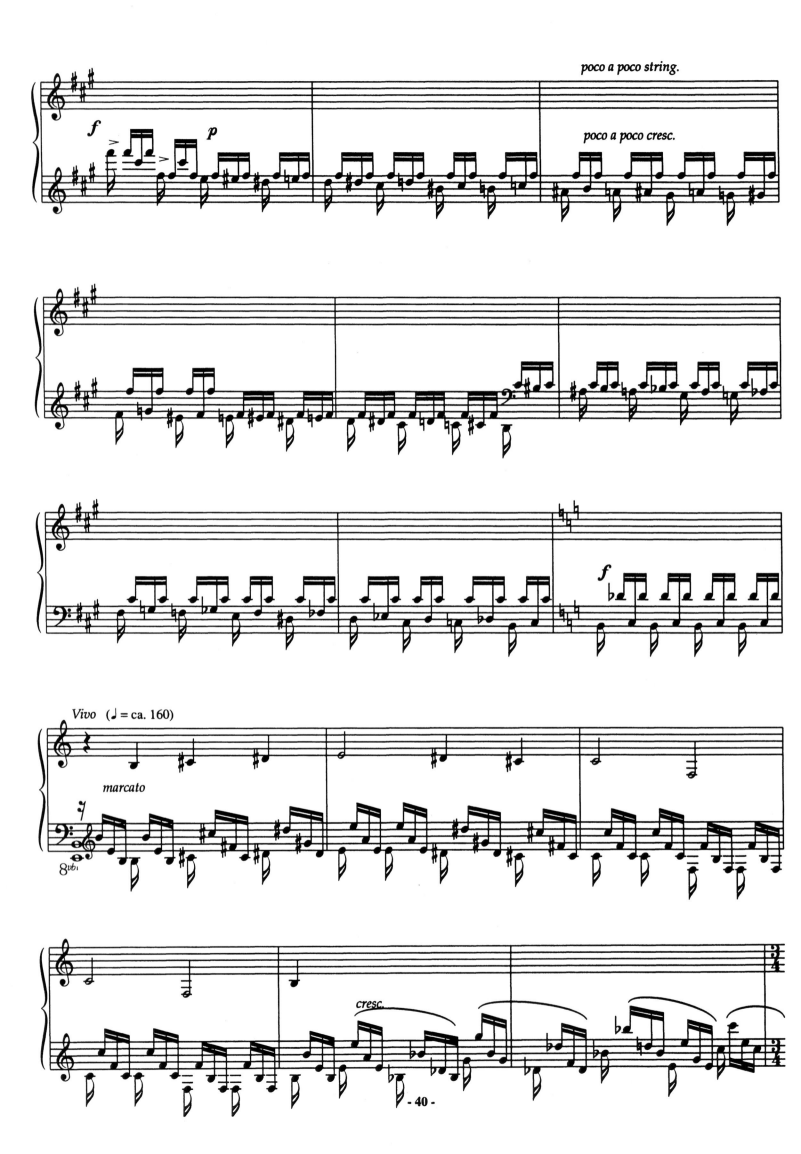